NATURE OF THE WORLD

Neil Morris

Introduction

This book takes us on a wonderful journey through six continents – North America, South America, Europe, Africa, Asia and Australasia. On each of these land masses we find a varying, colourful world of nature.

Animals live all over the world, from the frozen Arctic region to the warm, wet rainforests near the equator. They even manage to survive the baking heat of deserts such as the Sahara, the largest in the world. The animals in different habitats have developed very different ways of living, from the food they eat to the homes they look for or build themselves. Some animals live only in one region, such as the kangaroos and other marsupials of Australia. Others are found all over the world.

Plants vary across the continents according to the climate in which they live. The cactus can thrive in the dry desert, but would never survive an Arctic winter or a long rainy season. Very often the animals of a region depend on its plants for food. Many of the animals are hard to find in the wild, but we can get to know many of them in this book.

Tallest tree

Redwoods grow along the California coast of the USA. In the forest, these massive trees grow close together and shut out most of the sunlight. They grow up to 112 metres high and have trunks that are almost 4 metres in diameter. Their leaves are green needles that sometimes stay on the tree for several years. Since they are conifers, coast redwoods grow their seeds in large cones. The wood is soft and red, and the trees' thick bark is said to make them fire-resistant.

Did you know?

Some plants catch and feed on insects. Pitcher plants give off a sweet smell to lure an insect into their tube-like leaves. The insect falls into a pool of liquid at the bottom of the tube or "pitcher", and drowns. The liquid contains chemicals that digest it, making food for the plant. The Venus flytrap is another insectivorous plant.

Giant cactus

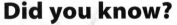

The Sonoran Desert stretches across the border between Arizona and California, in the USA, and northern Mexico. Three hundred different types of cactus grow there, including the largest in the world – the saguaro. This giant cactus sometimes grows over 17 metres tall. Gila woodpeckers often peck their way into saguaros to make their nest. And when they leave, tiny elf owls take their turn in the ready-made hole, safe from their enemies.

Did you know?

There are around 2000 different types of cacti in deserts and other dry regions around the world. The leaves or shoots of a cactus are spines, which help protect it from animals. Cacti have thick waxy outer layers and they store water in their spongy or hollow stems. Their roots spread out close to the surface of the ground, so that they can quickly absorb water after rare rainfall.

The Americas

Rainforests are always warm and wet, so it is not surprising that they are full of life. The biggest of all, the Amazon rainforest in South America, is no exception. While the jaguar prowls on the forest floor, sloths, spider monkeys and many other animals move through the branches above. But life goes on in the dry American deserts, too. Just look at the saguaro, the biggest of all the cactus plants.

SUGAR MAPLE
Canadians make maple syrup from the sap of this tree.

GARPIKE
A long-nosed freshwater fish of North America with strong jaws.

MANATEE
This sea cow comes to the surface to breathe, but never comes ashore.

COTTON
The cotton plant is grown for the soft fibre that covers its seeds.

AMERICAN ALLIGATOR
Some of these fierce creatures are over 5 m long.

MAIZE
This cereal grass, also called corn, is used as a vegetable and in breakfast cereals.

SAGUARO
This giant cactus grows up to 12 m high in southern USA and Mexico.

PRICKLY PEAR
This cactus has large flowers and produces pear-shaped fruit.

SLOTH
Sloths spend most of their time hanging from branches in the South American rainforest.

PIRANHA
A small river fish with razor-sharp teeth that hunts in large groups.

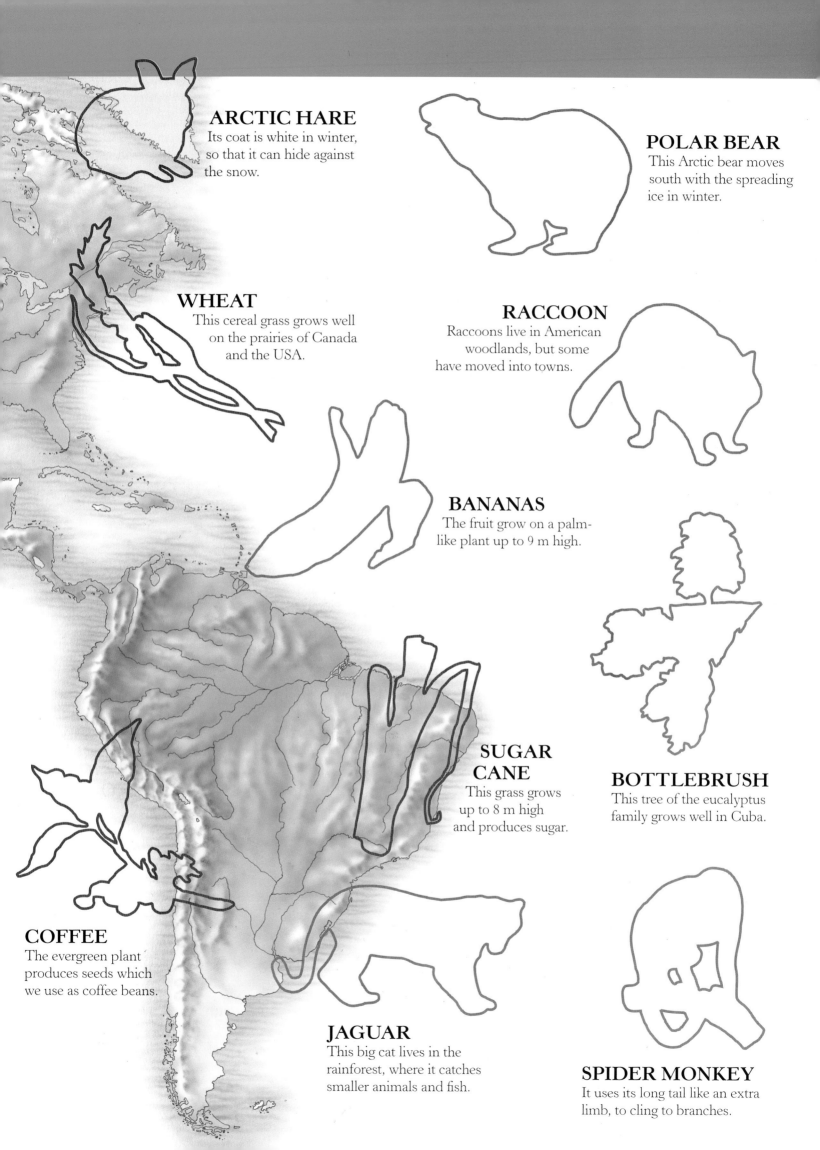

ARCTIC HARE
Its coat is white in winter, so that it can hide against the snow.

POLAR BEAR
This Arctic bear moves south with the spreading ice in winter.

WHEAT
This cereal grass grows well on the prairies of Canada and the USA.

RACCOON
Raccoons live in American woodlands, but some have moved into towns.

BANANAS
The fruit grow on a palm-like plant up to 9 m high.

SUGAR CANE
This grass grows up to 8 m high and produces sugar.

BOTTLEBRUSH
This tree of the eucalyptus family grows well in Cuba.

COFFEE
The evergreen plant produces seeds which we use as coffee beans.

JAGUAR
This big cat lives in the rainforest, where it catches smaller animals and fish.

SPIDER MONKEY
It uses its long tail like an extra limb, to cling to branches.

Poisonous frog

Arrow-poison frogs live in the forests of Central and South America. They are very poisonous, and local Native Americans traditionally extract the poison to use on the tips of their arrows. The frogs have brilliant colours, which warn enemies of danger. Arrow-poison frogs are caring parents. About two weeks after the female has laid her eggs, the male frog carries the hatched tadpoles on his back to a water-filled plant or tree-hole. The female then feeds the tadpoles regularly until they turn into froglets.

Did you know?

Brazilian wandering spiders are the most poisonous spiders in the world. Tarantulas are poisonous too. Their venom is fatal to the small insects on which they feed. Tarantulas have large bodies, with long, hairy legs. Some legends say that a person bitten by a tarantula should dance until they are worn out, to sweat the poison out of their body.

Poisonous snake

The king cobra of India and south-east Asia is the world's longest poisonous snake, growing up to 5.5 metres in length. When the cobra is frightened or excited, loose skin around its head can spread out to form a wide hood, which makes it look even more scary. Cobras can climb trees and swim if they have to. If they are threatened, for example by a mongoose, cobras sometimes lie still and pretend to be dead, until the danger has passed.

Did you know?

Sea snakes found in the Timor Sea off north-west Australia are more poisonous than any land snake. They spend their whole lives in water, and have a paddle-shaped tail which helps them swim. They are up to 1.5 metres long, and use their poisonous fangs to kill eels and small fish. They come to the surface regularly to breathe air.

The Americas

Coffee

Maize

Cotton

Saguaro

Prickly pear

Wheat

Banana

Bottlebrush

Sugar maple

Sugar cane

The Americas

Arctic hare

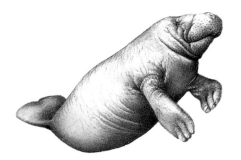

Manatee

Spider monkey

American alligator

Polar bear

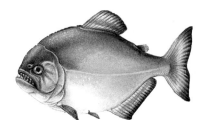

Piranha

Garpike

Sloth

Jaguar

Raccoon

Europe and Africa

Pine

Red fox

Sunflowers

Edelweiss

Grapes

Wild boar

Poppy

Badger

Fallow deer

Otter

Europe and Africa

Baobab

Wildebeest

Date palm

Elephant

Cheetah

Zebra

Kokerboom

Acacia

Traveller's tree

Lion

Asia and Australasia

Rice

Giant panda

Tea

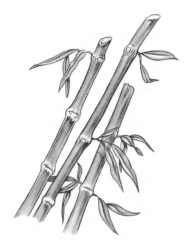

Baboon

Cedar

Tiger

Bamboo

Indian rhino

Larch

Tapir

Asia and Australasia

Kauri pine

Marsupial mole

Coconut

Kangaroo

Manuka

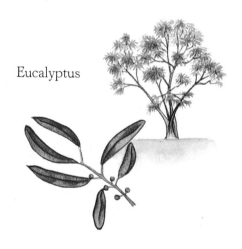

Eucalyptus

Dingo

Macrozamia

Thorny devil

Wombat

Vital statistics

Most endangered mammals

1	Tasmanian wolf	?
1	Halcon fruit bat	?
1	Ghana fat mouse	?
4	Kouprey (ox)	10
5	Javan rhinoceros	50
6	Iriomote cat	60
7	Black lion tamarin (monkey)	130
8	Pygmy hog	150
9	Tamaraw (water buffalo)	200
10	Indus river dolphin	400

The manatee is a large slow-moving mammal. It can stay underwater for up to 15 minutes and then comes to the surface to breathe air. On the coastline of the Caribbean Sea the manatee is being threatened by increases in tourism.

Did you know?

Most dolphins swim in salty oceans, but there are freshwater species in some of the world's big rivers, the Amazon in South America, the Chang Jiang in China and the Ganges and Indus in south Asia. All these dolphins are in danger of extinction, and some parts of the rivers have been made into reserves. The dolphins all have long, slender beaks and poor eyesight. They find their way about by sending out high-pitched sounds that bounce off things and make an echo.

World's food crops (in millions of tonnes)

Did you know?

Sugar cane plants probably grew wild on the island of New Guinea thousands of years ago. They were so highly valued that people traded them for goods, and traders carried sugar cane throughout the rest of the world. Europeans first saw sugar cane in India about 2300 years ago. European explorers carried the plants to the Caribbean and South America 500 years ago.

1	Sugar cane	1041
2	Wheat	565
3	Rice	527
4	Maize	471
5	Potatoes	288
6	Sugar beet	282
7	Barley	170
8	Cassava	154
9	Sweet potatoes	124
10	Soya beans	111

Europe and Africa

Africa is famous for its wildlife, and the African grasslands in particular. People come from all over the world to see lions, elephants and zebras in their natural home. Most of these animals are now protected in national parks. In Europe there are fewer wide open spaces, and the typical animals are smaller. On both continents, the plants reflect the nature of the land.

PINE
This tree has long slender needles for leaves and produces its seeds in cones.

BADGER
Badgers live in underground setts and come out at night to feed.

EDELWEISS
This pretty flower of the daisy family grows wild in the Alps.

GRAPES
The fruit of vines are used to make wine and other drinks.

DATE PALM
This tree grows in oases and produces sugary fruit.

RED FOX
Some foxes have moved into towns to find food.

LION
Unlike other big cats, lions live in groups called prides.

WILDEBEEST
Also called the gnu, this large antelope travels huge distances to find fresh grassland and water.

TRAVELLER'S TREE
This Madagascan tree looks like a giant fan. Its seeds are used for food.

FALLOW DEER
These European deer live in open woodland, and the males grow antlers.

OTTER
Otters live near rivers and lakes and spend much of their time in the water.

WILD BOAR
It uses its snout for rooting around in its woodland home.

POPPY
Corn or field poppies grow wild and are also popular with gardeners.

SUNFLOWERS
These tall flowers grow up to 3 m high, and their seeds are used to make oil.

ACACIA
This spiny, flat-topped tree gives some shade on the grassland.

ELEPHANT
African elephants live together in herds, led by an old female.

ZEBRA
This member of the horse family is best known for its striped coat.

KOKERBOOM
Also called the quiver tree, it stores water and grows well on dry land.

CHEETAH
This big cat's sleek body is built for speed.

BAOBAB
The trunk of this tropical tree swells up when it has water to drink.

Asia and Australasia

Both continents have animals that live nowhere else on Earth. Tigers are the world's largest big cats, and the biggest of all are the Siberian tigers that live in the Far East of Asia. Australia is famous for its marsupials – animals which carry their young in pouches. Kangaroos, wombats and koalas are all marsupials, and there is even a marsupial mole.

CEDAR
These tall trees often grow to a height of 40 m.

BABOON
These big monkeys spend most of their time on the ground.

TIGER
Unlike most cats, the biggest of the big cats is a good swimmer.

INDIAN RHINO
This rhinoceros is big and heavy, but can run at up to 40 kph.

COCONUT
The coconut palm has huge nuts which take a year to ripen.

TEA
Tea is made from the dried leaves and shoots of this evergreen plant.

WOMBAT
This burrowing animal spends most of the day in its underground home.

MACROZAMIA
This Australian tree looks like a palm but is a member of the cycad family.

THORNY DEVIL
This strange-looking lizard lives in the Australian desert

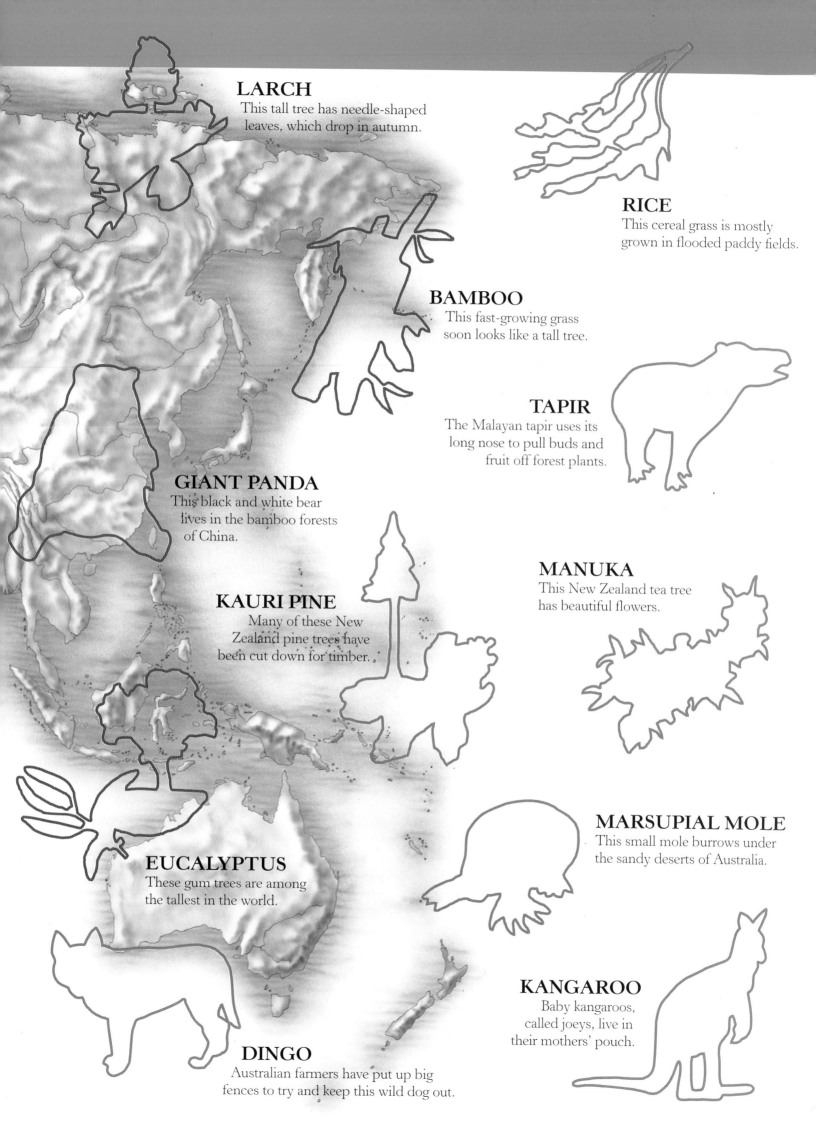

LARCH
This tall tree has needle-shaped leaves, which drop in autumn.

RICE
This cereal grass is mostly grown in flooded paddy fields.

BAMBOO
This fast-growing grass soon looks like a tall tree.

TAPIR
The Malayan tapir uses its long nose to pull buds and fruit off forest plants.

GIANT PANDA
This black and white bear lives in the bamboo forests of China.

MANUKA
This New Zealand tea tree has beautiful flowers.

KAURI PINE
Many of these New Zealand pine trees have been cut down for timber.

EUCALYPTUS
These gum trees are among the tallest in the world.

MARSUPIAL MOLE
This small mole burrows under the sandy deserts of Australia.

DINGO
Australian farmers have put up big fences to try and keep this wild dog out.

KANGAROO
Baby kangaroos, called joeys, live in their mothers' pouch.

Design: First Edition
Art Director: Clare Sleven
Project Manager: Susanne Grant
Production Assistant: Ian Paulyn
Colour Reproduction: DPI Colour Ltd.
Illustrations: Gillian Platt, Alison Winfield

This is a Parragon Book
This edition published in 2001
Parragon, Queen Street House, 4 Queen Street, Bath, BA1 1HE

2 4 6 8 10 9 7 5 3

Produced by Miles Kelly Publishing Ltd,
Bardfield Centre, Great Bardfield, Essex, CM7 4SL

British Library Cataloguing-in-Publication Data
A catalogue record for this book is available from the British Library

ISBN 0 75253 271 5

Printed in Italy
by STIGE Turin